Cave Drawings

Cave Drawings

Barbara Ann Carle

Cave Drawings
Copyright © 2017 by BARBARA ANN CARLE

All rights reserved. No part of this publication maybe reproduced, stored in a retrieval system, or transmitted in any form or by any means, electronic, mechanical, photocopying, recording or otherwise, without the written permission of the author.

USBS # 978-0-9976261-0-0

Cover Designed – Carnes Group Creative
Cover Drawing - Scott Edwin Carle

Versions of the below poems originally appeared in the following publication:

In 2008, "The Viking Ship" was published in Sol Magazine. In 2009, "The Battle" won the Ted O. Badger Award, the Poetry Society of Texas. The Texas Poetry Calendar, published "The Hunt" in 2011, "Twenty Bucks" in 2012 and "Your Favorite Boots" in 2013. "Flight of the Flamingo" appeared in the Mutabilis Press anthology "Untameable City in 2015.

Published by Church Avenue Press
Houston, Texas

Dedication

For thirty-five years, my husband Ed and I had the joy of watching our son Scott grow into a wonderful husband, father, and successful, respected Assistant Principal.

For the last two years of his life, Scott taught us the meaning of courage and unbelievable bravery. During his illness, his sole concern was for the people he loved the most. His final days were spent preparing everyone for his death and enlisting the aid of others to help care for his wife and children after he was gone.

Ed and I may have taught Scott how to live but he taught us how to die with dignity and a sensitivity that far surpassed what we could have imagined. He was all a parent could desire in a son, and we were proud to call him our friend.

Letter to Demeter

Winter lays bare the landscape
turns the world gray
undresses the trees
and I think of you

Your search
for your daughter Persephone
kidnapped by Hades

Your torment and sorrow so great
you darkened the world
until the gods came to your aid

And I ask
If I mourn long enough
hard enough
will God, like Zeus
take pity and
return my son?

Or will this pen
have to be enough.

Barbara Ann Carle

Contents

Letter to Demeter
Cave Drawings   1
Bluebonnet Time   2
Babysitting   4
Night Ride   8
Self Portrait: Pen and Ink   10
Your Favorite Boots   11
Family Man   12
Twenty Bucks   14
Fear   15
Battle   16
Again   18
Mimic   20
Rose   23
Your Father   24

Long Ride Home	26
Hope	29
A Single Yellow Rose	30
Farewell Christopher Robin	32
The Wait	36
Sixty Seconds	38
Late One Saturday Afternoon	40
Let Us Pray	44
The Stranger	46
The Prayer	48
Infinite Possibilities	49
Last Goodbye	50
Aftermath	53
Art of War	54
The Viking Ship	56

Sacred Tantrum	58
Nightmare	60
Next to Godliness	62
The Sisterhood	64
The Hunt	65
Unannounced	66
On the Wing	68
Flight of the Flamingo	70
A New Day	72
Melanoma	75
Acknowledgement	79

Scott
Summer of 1992

Introduction

I've led a charmed life. I was born and grew up in New York City, one of the most exciting places in the world. In 1956, I met a tall, blond engineer named Ed Carle. We started dating, fell in love and married in 1959.

A year later, in July of 1960, our first son, Scott was born. A little over two years later, our first daughter, Paula came into our lives. When I was about seven months pregnant with our third child, Ed came home from work early and said "You know Grumman is building the Lunar Modular. They are going to put a man on the moon, and they want me on the team. How would you like to move to Houston, Texas?" I wasn't too happy at first but it was a great opportunity for Ed. And the plan was we would only be gone for two years, three at the most.

So, in 1965, soon after our second daughter, Melissa was born, we sold our house on Long Island, loaded our young family into our new station wagon and headed south. Ed loved his new job, the children thrived, the Company extended our stay, the Space Program made history, and, in 1969 our second son, Glen was born.

The years flew by. Our three oldest children married. Our youngest graduated college and was gainfully employed.

In 1991 Scott and his wife Carolyn presented us with a beautiful new granddaughter, Rose. Three years later, Ed accepted a short-term assignment in San Augustine, Florida and was seriously considering retirement in the near future. Life was good.

One evening, while Ed and I were busy preparing for our move, Scott, just thirty-three years old, and his wife, Carolyn, walked through the back door. He sat next to me on the blue plaid couch in the family room, took my hand, and said, "Mom, I have cancer" and everything changed.

Cave Drawings

We don't draw on the walls, son.
We color on paper so I can hang them
on the refrigerator.

Your huge blue Picasso eyes
look puzzled
You smile
and never put crayon to wall again

But two years later
we decide to paint your closet
I lift an armload of clothes
and uncover a stick figure mural
houses, trees, mountains
clouds, the sun
and a giant blue lake with a sailboat

I didn't realize
your talent needed a canvas
larger than 8 ½ x 11.

Bluebonnet Time

You climbed off the bus
The sun bounced
off your golden hair
your toothless grin
greeted my smile

Yellow construction paper
clutched to your chest
You can't see it till we get home.

Popcorn dyed bright blue
crooked stem
ragged leaves
cut with blunt nose scissors
Name scrawled in first grade letters

It's the State flower.
you instructed your Yankee mom

It hung on the kitchen cork board
until the edges curled
I stored it in a plastic box
along with all your childhood drawings
choir programs
1st place ribbons from art shows
football, baseball and basketball
team pictures
and everything else I've lost.

Babysitting

*Mrs. Weitz said not to worry
about the poison berries.*

What poison berries?

*The ones the baby ate
while you were gone.*

You are thirteen years old
and calmly sit at the end
of the kitchen table

*What! Where did the baby
get poison berries?*

*In the backyard
on that bush over there.*

You point out
the kitchen window
towards a row of shrubs

*I told you to keep him
in the house?*

*He kept pestering me
to go outside. You know how he gets.*

You shrug your shoulders
and frown

*So when he ate the berry
you took him to Mrs. Weitz's?*

*Well, first I rinsed his mouth out
with water
then we went to Dr. Haynie's house.
He tasted some of the berry juice
said it was so bitter
Glen wouldn't have swallowed it.*

How did Dr. Haynie taste the berry juice?

*I brought some of the berries with me
in a paper cup.*

I look across the table at your Dad
who proudly beams at you
In the family room I hear
cartoon music playing
on the television
three-year-old Glen
and eight-year-old Melissa laughing

Then I took him to see Mrs. Weitz.
She used to be a nurse and knows
all about gardening.
She said to tell you
not to worry. She recognized
the berries and said they aren't poisonous.

I look from you
to your Dad

Ed, you were due home any minute.
I had to pick up Glen's prescription.
I was gone less than thirty minutes.

He smiles
I think Scott did a great job.

Night Ride

I keep on thinking bout you,
Sister Golden Hair surprise
America quietly harmonizes

Eighteen years old
behind the wheel of our Winnebago
you smile
Every time I hear that line, Mom
I think of Melissa
my sister golden hair so fine.

Everyone is asleep
I sit up front
and keep you company

Isolated in a tunnel of black
we sail the deserted back road
headed towards midnight
and Canton, Texas

We talk about you starting college
next month
your latest girl friend
make plans for your trip to San Antonio
and together
we softly sing the chorus.

Self Portrait: Pen and Ink

You lay your sketch pad
on the kitchen table
ask *What do you think?*

Your head is covered
in intricate feathered owls
falcons and hawks
I smile
It is so you

Your face is lined and wrinkled
Why did you make yourself so ancient?
You just laugh

Fifteen years later
in the hospital, you say
Good thing I drew that picture Mom.
Now you know what I'd look like
if I had gotten old.

Your Favorite Boots

Scuffed pointed toes
brown snake skin tops
hand-tooled leather sides
worn down heels
hidden in a corner
of my closet

Prized possession
bought with your own money
at the huge flea market in Canton
Worn with tight Wrangler jeans
or your Sunday best

Once a year I take them out
circle polish slowly
into every crevice
brush them till they gleam

I should get rid of them
they've been empty so long
yet I secret them away
Maybe next year.

Family Man

You met Carolyn
fell in love
and got married

You gifted us
with three instant grandchildren
Just add water, mix
and love

Quiet, dark haired
four-year-old Joshua
you taught him
how to play basketball
ride a bike
You shared his love of books

You watched "Sleeping Beauty"
a thousand times
with exuberant, golden haired
three-year-old twins
Sarah and Emily
You coached their softball teams
and taught them how to roller skate

You learned Sarah's language
your hands tossed words
through the air
entering her silent world
She followed you
everywhere you went

Trips to The State Capitol
Astro-world
Disney World

You held your precious newborn
Rose
taught how to talk and sing
Together you flew with Peter Pan
and spun in magic Teacups

For almost ten years
you loved them
and made them laugh

You were torn from their lives
way too soon.

Twenty Bucks

You trained that black lab from a pup
prepared her for the big day

Your friend Jeff said
Bet ya twenty bucks
once we're in the marsh
she won't retrieve a thing.

Her year-old paws
charged through the tall grass
feathered prize gently cradled
between her jaws

She proudly deposited
each slobbered find
at your feet
then danced with joy

In the back of the pick-up
on the way home
she ate all the ducks

You never did collect that twenty.

Fear

Tiny tentacles
creeping across my chest
around my back
Mom, I have cancer.

Slowly wrapping
around my heart
weaving between my ribs
There's an 80% chance it won't reoccur.

Growing, twisting and knotting
snaking over my shoulders
coiling around my spine
Mom, I have a lump.

Constricting my vocal chords
crushing my diaphragm
clawing your way into my stomach
It's spread to my lungs.

Then
He's gone.
Your grip unwinding
releasing me to unbearable sorrow.

Battle

I walked the floor at night
when you had colic
studied Dr. Spock
bandaged every cut and scrape
held my breath
while you played football

So why can't I fix this
find a remedy
conjure up a spell

I sit with you
while you wait
for your Radiation appointment
talk to another mother
Her daughter has breast cancer

She whispers
It's so hard to watch
your child battle this disease.
And I reply
I just wish it was me.

You hear me
and your anger flares
hot and fast
Don't ever say that again.

*Do you think I wouldn't trade places
with you in a minute?* I lash back

We both turn away

The first cross words shared
since you became a man

I reach for your hand
you squeeze my fingers
They call your name

You stand
and leave the room.

Again

You carry your pillow
blue denim quilt
and portable CD player

I carry a black gym bag
with your CDs, tee shirts, shorts
comb, tooth paste, deodorant
slippers and some books

We board the elevator
Operations, treatments
We know the routine

Six days of interferon and interleukin
will poison your body
pain, nausea, diarrhea

If you sleep
then I will
slouch down
into the brown leather chair
count my beads and pray
Hail Mary, full of grace

3 p.m. is Batman time
propped up on pillows
your artist eye shows me
things I do not see

Shading, crosshatching
bringing your favorite
cartoon character to life

Day seven
you drag yourself out of bed
You'll do anything to go home today
instead of tomorrow

So we walk
round and round
the nurses' station

The doctor warned you
It's fifty times worse
than the worse flu you've ever had.
and now you laugh
He was way too optimistic.

Finally, release papers in hand
we head for the elevator again

The nurse calls
Good night Mr. Carle
see you next month.

Mimic

One morning I found you
sitting on the edge of the bed
swinging your thin legs
staring at the floor
Are you looking for something?

Just my Blue Suede Shoes.
you said in your Elvis voice
All day long
every question answered
with another of his song titles

Another day you were Bugs Bunny
and asked the oncologist
What's up Doc?
He never did know quite
what to make of you

And then there were the stories

*Remember the day
you sent Glen and me to the store.
He was swinging a 5-lb. bag
of potatoes in the parking lot.
It broke and some lady drove her Cadillac
over them. They all went pop, pop, pop.
and she called us juvenile delinquents.*

*The time Glen and I went
to Tae Kwon Do
and Melissa's pink bikini underpants
were stuck to the back of his gi.
Glen got so mad and then
we laughed so hard
they almost sent us home.*

The day
I stood in the corner of your room
with some friends
whispering and softly crying
I checked to see
if you were still asleep

Eyes closed, you raised
your frail arms into the air
and with your long
graceful fingers, in sign language
spelled out
Stop sniveling,
you're raising the humidity in here.

Every day
you made me laugh
Another story, another joke
no matter how sick, how tired
or how unbearable your pain.

Rose

You help her
chubby four-year-old fingers
struggle with blunt nosed scissors

Father and daughter
cut seven strips
of colored construction paper
One for each day
of another hospital stay

Together you weave two chains
one for her room
one to hang over your hospital bed

You place a call each night
at her bedtime
and you each cut off one link.
Three more days till Daddy comes home.

The next afternoon she calls, crying
You gently talk to her
calm her down and hang up

Laughing you say
She cut up all the links.
Call the doctor
tell him I have to go home.

Your Father

He un-wrapped the blue receiving blanket
    counted your ten fingers and toes

played peek-a-boo
    helped you learn to walk

wrapped your chubby fingers around a baseball
    taught you how to throw that ball

ran behind your two-wheeler
    until it was time to let go

listened to your multiplication tables
    told you how girls were different

helped you with your Science Fair Project
    you won second place

helped you put minnows on your fishing hook
    so you could teach your children

showed you how to shave
    how to tie a Winsor knot

taught you how to drive
    how to change a flat tire

tutored you in trigonometry
    rebuilt your carburetor

sat by your bedside at night
    when you were in the hospital

held your hand when you were sick
    and when you were afraid

was your rock
    and mine too

embraced me when I cried
    kept our family strong.

The Long Ride Home

I

We ride home in silence
The air in the car
poisoned by the final diagnosis
three to six months
But you decide to try one last drug
so it's back into the hospital

II

I need to make a stop, Mom.
How many times have I heard
those words?
  I have to go to Academy
  Texas Art Supply
  Barnes & Noble.
  Can we go to Baskin & Robbins?
Where to now?
I need to stop at the funeral parlor
and make the arrangements.

III

I feel my heart shatter
into tiny slivers of glass
and I take your hand
No, son, that's our job, not yours.
Are you sure?
Yes, I'm sure.

I want to be cremated.
you laugh
You know how claustrophobic I am.
Scatter my ashes
in the Guadalupe River
near my favorite fly fishing spot.

IV

Your large hand crushes
my smaller one
as you turn away
Thanks, Mom.

I watch you
watch the miles and time
fly by the window
You don't let go
until we're home

V

But that summer day
when your ashes
cradled by a gentle wind
rode the rapids one last time
I wasn't there
It was not my choice
The wishes of a young wife
for privacy

VI

So this summer
family and friends
will climb down
the banks
near the Grist Mill
sprinkle red rose petals
into the icy waters
of the river
feast on Snicker bars
laugh, cry
and wish you Godspeed.

Hope

I would do anything for you
slink down a dark alleyway
to meet you
grab my fifty-dollar baggie
hurry home

I would slowly snort
razor blade lines
of your white powder
await the rush

You are the only thing
that kills the hospital smell
dulls the steady beep, beep
of machines

You whisper
*He looks so much better today
not so gaunt.*
and I can see you're right

Your voice echoes in my ear
*Don't worry, he'll be fine
He can't die, he's too young.*
and I believe

I listen to your song
memorize each word
You silence my every doubt
as I clutch you tighter.

A Single Yellow Rose

It was there in the center
of a pink and red bouquet
brought to the hospital
by a group of college kids
from all over Texas
who came to say good-bye
to their favorite
high school teacher

They gathered around your bed
laughing about their antics in school
trips to conventions in Austin
year-end pool parties at our house

What do you like best about college?
you asked
History
Math
Girls
English
Computer Science
Free ice cream

What are you majoring in?
Education
Finance
Education
Computers
Education
Education

You kept it light, joking
knowing when
to send them on their way
You ought to go home now.
Spend some time with your folks
before you head back to school.

As they walked passed your bed
headed out into the cold
February rain
I saw tears shining in their eyes

Later, I read the card
attached to the flowers

Mr. Carle,
You, like the yellow rose,
compliment all who surround you.

Farewell Christopher Robin

It's 7 a.m.
time to relieve your brother
On Friday nights
he would take the night shift
so Dad could take a break

I exit the elevator
see him pacing by your room
He sees the panic in my eyes
smiles and gives the O.K. sign

Arm around my shoulder
he says *Scott's fine Mom.*
He was restless during the night
but we talked and I read to him
until he dozed off.
He's sound asleep now.
I was just stretching my legs.
After a hug and a kiss
I send him home to get some rest.

I tiptoe into your room
sit in the brown leather chair
and watch you sleep

They wake you
with the food tray you wave off
I tempt you with dry toast and a Sprite

How was your night? I ask

*Not too bad. I couldn't sleep
but Glen was great.
We talked and talked.
You know what he did?*

*He read me Winnie the Pooh
pulled his chair up close to the bed
leaned his head on my pillow
so I could see the pictures. We had so much fun.
Remember how he always wanted me
to read him Pooh?*

I remember
I think I'll rest for awhile Mom.

You close your eyes
I close mine

I can see you
five years old
snuggled beside me on the couch
your blue eyes puzzled
Why is Eeyore always so unhappy Momma?
Some people just can't find things to be happy about. I say
You smile *I'm glad we're not like that.*

Nine years old
you sit with Paula on the right
Melissa on the left
You all laugh as Piglet and Pooh
go round and round
trying to track a Woozle

Thirteen years old
you sit at the kitchen table
four-year-old Glen stands
holding the book in one hand
the other hand on his hip
Come on Scott, read it one more time
then I promise I'll go to bed.

As a father, sitting on the floor
reading and signing
while Joshua, Emily and Sarah giggle
as Rabbit tries to push Pooh
through his front door

With three-year-old Rose
sprawled in your lap
This is daddy's favorite book, honey.
It's about a little bear
who does funny, silly things
and then thinks of very smart things
whenever his friends are in trouble.

I see two grown men
heads together
one drawn and so desperately ill
the other young and virile
smiling as Pooh struggles to free his head
from the honey jar

Sharing one last
        bedtime story.

The Wait

Rain drops pepper the window
I chart their journey down the pane
Our lives held captive by these walls

Painting
of a sun-filled meadow
your blue denim quilt
soft music from your favorite CD

None of these
can combat
the constant beep of machines
the smell of alcohol
disinfectant and sweat
yours and mine

We've learned to ignore
life outside our door
the murmur of voices
squeaky wheels of a wayward cart
doctors being paged

I read to you
we talk
we pray

As you sleep
I watch
the black minute hand
on the giant wall clock
slowly march
towards a time
I cannot face
while the rhythm of my heart beats

Wait. Wait. Wait.
Please, don't take him yet.

I am surprised when you speak
Mom, please don't let this ruin your life.
It's too short to waste. Promise me.

Tear drops blur the room
as I softly whisper
I'll try, sweetheart
I'll try.

Sixty Seconds

I toss my empty coffee cup
into the stainless-steel trash can
near the nurse's station
and head back to your room

I stop
bend my knees
I try to pick up my feet
but I have waded
into a puddle of Super Glue

My mind screams
I can't go back.
I won't watch you suffer any more.

You are my first born
I kept you safe
I saw you at My death bed
Not this
I can't help you die

Shame weeps from every pore
rivulets run down my legs
and set me free
I hurry to your side
I stay until the end

It was just one minute
out of thirty-five years
It haunts me still.

Late One Saturday Afternoon

It wasn't planned
no visitors
girlfriend
spouses
It was just the six of us

We reminisced
laughed
You guys look so tired. Paula said
Go get something to eat
in a real restaurant
not the hospital cafeteria.
The four of us will hang out here
until you get back.

Ed and I picked a corner table
cried together
ate a real meal together
made plans for Scott's
pending release

When we got back to the hospital
all of the kids
were laughing and joking

The sun went down
Melissa headed out first
hugs and kisses all around

Ed was spending the night
Next Glen, Paula and I
said goodnight

I slid down in the back seat
of the car
closed my eyes

Glen's voice was excited
Melissa was great, Mom.
She said
Let's all join hands.

*We gathered around Scott's bed
and she started telling him
what a great brother he was,
how much he meant to her.
Then Paula took a turn
did the same
and then I did too.*

*I never would have
thought of that on my own.
I wouldn't have known
where to start.* Paula said
Soon we were praying and crying.

*Then Scott starting telling us
what pests we were
when we were little.* Glen said
*How I broke his model airplanes,
Paula kept stealing his Hot Wheel,
and Missy always had to sit next
to him everywhere we went.*

*We were all laughing so hard.
When I see Missy tomorrow I'm
gonna thank her.*

I closed my eyes again
listened to wipers on the windshield
and James Taylor
on the radio
softly singing
Shower the people you love with love

I tried to visualize the scene
around his bed
and wished
I could have been there.

Let Us Pray

Early one Sunday morning
a fellow teacher
and her pastor
from the First Baptist Antioch Church
his ancient Bible's spine covered
with gray duct tape
came to your room
to pray
God, please send us a cure.

Three ladies dressed in red, teal
and plum colored suits
matching shoes
wonderful large hats covered with flowers
feathers and ribbons
Members of their church choir
their heavenly acappella voices
floating down the hall
attracted a huge crowd
outside your room

Noon time one of your student's fathers
an Episcopal priest
brought you a giant flower arrangement
and prayed for your total recovery

My friend Linda
and her Mormon Church's
healing group
anointed your forehead with oil
blessed and prayed over you

That night
our Catholic priest came
heard your confession
and gave you communion

You were so tired
slumped down in the bed
and seemed asleep
until you smiled and said

Hey Mom, if you could go round up
a Rabbi,
a Buddhist monk
and a Hindu priest
I think we will have covered
all the bases today.

The Stranger

I don't believe we've met before
really met
We've crossed paths
but your visits were quick, swift

Then one day you showed up
and decided to stay awhile
coming and going at will

Each time you left
I was so relieved
I hated you whenever you returned

You made yourself comfortable
in his living room
lounging on the couch
feet up on the cushions

In the doctor's waiting room
hands behind your head
you sprawled in a chair

You elbowed your way
into his hospital room
wouldn't leave
You followed him wherever he went
hovering over his shoulder
breathing down his neck

I could see you in the shadows
feel you in the air
Silently I screamed
Go away. Go away.
You pretended you couldn't hear me

I prayed you would disappear
Leave us alone.

But I forgot

When you finally left
       you took him with you.

The Prayer

It rained every day
that February

I sat huddled
in the passenger seat
holding a paper sack
hamburgers and fries
I was so hungry
but too tired to chew

At home after a few bites
I threw myself into bed
Clutching my rosary
I admitted defeat
You had suffered too much
Thy will be done
Please take him in his sleep.

Two days later, at 3:30 a.m.
your wife called
said *He's gone.*

Why did God answer THAT prayer
so quickly?

Infinite Possibilities

I didn't know
tomorrow wouldn't come

When I kissed you goodbye
said *I'll see you in the morning.*

I didn't know we wouldn't share
another day

What would we have said?
What would we have done?

If I had never left.

Last Goodbye

I stand wedged in the corner of your room
watching you sleep.
Your wife sits in a brown leather chair
reading a book. I listen
to your labored breathing,
watching your chest rise, fall, rise, fall
then stop.

I step forward, try to scream
No, not yet.
but my throat is closed.

Alarms sound and ghost-like people
move around your bed. But you
and I are all alone.

Suddenly you sit up,
looking strong.
Your hated dark brown,
post-chemo hair is gone,
golden blond waves are back.

Your face is fuller.
Your blue eyes are clear and bright.

You leap up on the bed,
dressed in navy blue Dockers,
light blue short-sleeve shirt
and brown loafers.
You take a huge healthy breath,
and I feel your relief.

You laugh and begin jumping
on your giant hospital trampoline.
The ceiling and walls melt away.
We are on the roof.
The cold, February, rain-filled air
blurs the late-night skyline
and whips through my hair.
I feel no chill.

You run and leap into the air,
go higher and higher into the sky,
spread your arms and soar.
I spin around in circles,
watching you climb, roll and dive,
just like your favorite birds.
You weave between the skyscrapers,
your laughter echoing off their walls.

I spread my arms, run along the roof top
and your joy vibrates through my skin.

You make one final pass,
then fly straight up
into the ink black sky.

How can I not let you go?

Aftermath

Cheated, cheated
my silent chant
echoes through
the empty rooms

The doctor said
You have three to six months.
Go home, enjoy the time
you have left.
But you wanted to try one last drug
that was six short weeks ago

No one last trip to Corpus Christi
No filmed messages for your four-year-old
daughter, Rose
No one last giant dinner party
No one last Easter or spring break

Now there's
no place to go
nothing to do

So we sit on the couch
and stare.

The Art of War

The battle
for the last leaf on the tree
raged outside my window
Three golden warriors
vied for the final honor

The first, felled by howling winds
the second, torrential rain
Hanging by a thread
the victor reigned supreme
two glorious days

And I thought of you

How valiantly you clung
to the tree of life

Battered by three operations
radiation and months
of interferon and interleukin treatments
nausea, weight loss and horrible pain

You had so much more
to give
But melanoma
rarely accepts defeat

So one cold winter night
while the world slept
plucked by the hand of God
you fell too soon
and simply blew away.

The Viking Ship

When you were sick
you built a Viking ship
lovingly carved of white wood
It was intricate and beautiful

The dragon-headed prow
faced the future
Three hand carved shields
decorated port and starboard

You fashioned tiny people
out of white paper
On long strips you wrote
thoughts and deeds
you wanted to set free
You rolled them up
tied them with twine
and placed them in the hull

I never read your scrolls

You planned a Viking funeral
to sail upon your favorite lake
to set your ship afire
and release your worldly cares

In the hospital
in your last days, you said
Mom, don't forget to burn my ship.

Dearest Scott
please forgive me
After I lost you
I couldn't burn your ship

It is a part of you
I can't let go.

Sacred Tantrum

I wish that I could pitch a fit
fling myself on the floor
unafraid of broken bones
punch and kick my hands and feet

Rip out all my hair
smash every glass and dish
break all the windows
run until I drop

Scream as loud as possible
with no intention of stopping
allow tears and snot to fall where they may
Angry child, mad at God the Father

Wail, *How could you do this to me?*
You took my son
and won't give him back.
It's not fair. I Was A Good Girl.

I wish I could let the venom spew
I don't love You anymore.
I hate You.
I'll never speak to You again.

Hold my breath until I turn blue
demand I get my way
He was mine. Give him back.
Lie on the floor, hiccup my tears away

Glorious release of anger and frustration
abandon all self-control
regain the innocence of my youth
believe my will, not His, be done

But I am no longer a child
So here I sit
holding fast to faith and trust
that God will guide my way.

Nightmare

I claw my way
towards consciousness
banish the choke hold
of sleep

Why must you
come to me
gaunt and sick?
Eyes pleading
Help me Mom
I'm afraid.

Why can't you
visit me
strong
and healthy?

Why can't I remember you
playing football
camping on the Guadalupe
fly fishing
or playing games with your children?

Sunrise
drenched in sweat
I vacate my bed
unwilling to revisit
your haunting blue eyes.

Next to Godliness

Allspice, Anise, Basil, Bay Leaf, Cinnamon,
Cloves, Garlic, Ginger

4:30 a.m.
I stand in the kitchen
in my robe and slippers
and realize what I'm doing

How I wish I could pick up the phone
and call you
Mom, I know you would say
I think you're losing it.

I sit on the couch
smother my laughter
in the blue throw pillow

I've organized each closet
straightened all the cabinets
scrubbed the tile floors
the bathrooms
vacuumed every rug
over and over

But no matter how hard I clean
I can't bring you back.

The Sisterhood
A pantoum.

How do we survive it?
Mothers who have lost our children
Left to cradle a shattered heart
A sisterhood of pain

Mothers who have lost our children
We cry *It should have been me.*
A sisterhood of pain
We crave one more embrace

We cry *It should have been me.*
How do we go on?
We crave one more embrace
Another day, another year

How do we go on?
Fill the hollow space inside
Another day, another year
How do we survive it?

The Hunt

I watch the jagged V
wobble across
the hazy morning sky

For just a moment
I hear your laugh
and see your smile

Your camo-clad ghost
shouldering giant sacks of decoys
into your brother's black pick-up

While your long-lost
black Lab, Moe
dances in the driveway.

Unannounced

No one invited you into my home today
No one asked if you could call

You just showed up, unannounced
intent on ruining my day

It's not that I didn't expect you
February is peeking over my shoulder

It's just that you came early
caught me unaware

I can't exactly call you depression
After all, it's been twenty years

You're more a pain
that gnaws at my bone marrow

But I'm stronger now
I've learned to go on

I've survived the worst
haven't I?

So this year, I ushered you
into the closet

Locked the door
left you kicking and screaming

I picked up
my keys

Got in my car
and simply drove away.

On the Wing

I study the photograph.
A tall, majestic bronze statue
of St. Francis
arms outstretched
three metal sparrows in each palm.

He stands at the edge
of a murky gray pond
head and shoulders
decorated with a flock
of fluttering black birds.

I smile
and hear your voice.
Birds, Mama, birds!
Your chubby finger points
in the air. Your white
high-tops kick
the navy-blue stroller
with glee.

Your eyes were always
focused skyward.
Each Christmas, you devoured
a new Audubon book, memorizing
all their names, habitats
and plumage.

At age fifteen
you brought home an injured barn owl,
tried to save him
and cried when he died.

While teaching you to drive,
I scolded
Keep your eyes on the road.
You laughed,
But Mom, it's a red-tailed hawk.

In college you studied
art and ornithology.
You drew a self-portrait
with birds woven
throughout your hair.

And when you flew away,
I searched the stormy skies
and wept.

Flight of the Flamingo

I sip my morning coffee
in my 13th floor nest
up in the sky

A bright pink blur
streaks by my window
giant black tipped wings
labor to keep his oval body aloft
long spindly legs trailing
his curved neck and beak straining
into the wind

He circles above the trees
in Hermann Park
Is he an escapee from the zoo?
He heads toward the Galleria
a barren place for a water fowl

You would love my new
glass living room
We could sit on the couch
watch the birds soar and dive
enjoy our eye level view

You knew so much about them
their habitats
You could teach me all their names

I wish I could pick up the phone and call
Would you be as amazed as I?
Or would you say
He's not rare in Texas, Mom.
He's just lost.

A New Day

Dear Scott,

The crisp Autumn breeze whistles
between the open
sliding glass doors
and dances with the beige silk drapes

The first rays of peach and orange sunlight
blossom over the horizon
chasing away the shadows of night

The faint rumble
of early morning traffic
climbs up thirteen floors
quickens my pulse
as the city wakes

I step out on the balcony
spread my arms
embrace the new day

I send my morning prayers
into the universe
and smile

I walk into my study
past the bookcase

A shelf of anthologies and books
contain my work

I sit at my desk
This book ready for the printer
lays in my outbox

The new book
a collection of essays
about your life
ready for the proof reader

A new project
waits in my desk drawer

I think of you every day
but now, I am at peace

I remember that rainy January day
you and I alone
in your hospital room

I hear your voice
Don't let this ruin your life.

       I kept my promise.

           Love,
           Mom

Melanoma

For centuries, pale alabaster skin was considered an important component of female beauty. During the Victorian Era, white skin was so valued, ladies bleached their complexions with lemon or dandelion juice. Some even went so far as to use creams mixed with arsenic or mercury, which often would prove fatal.

Women's daytime fashion was designed to protect their bodies from the sun, featuring high collars and long sleeves. When going outside, ladies wore large hats or sunbonnets, gloves and they carried parasols. Pale skin was considered a sign of refinement and class distinction for both sexes. Only men who worked as laborers or women who could not afford domestic help were exposed to the sun and had tanned skin. White skin indicated the ability to spend extended time indoors.

For a short time, in the 1900's, lying in the sun was believed to be a cure for tuberculosis but that never proved to be successful.

In 1923, legend says, famed fashion icon, Coca Chanel was accidently sun burned while sailing on the Riviera. When she arrived back in Paris with a golden tan, woman believed this was a new beauty trend and immediately began to tan their skin. It was also the "Roaring Twenties", and woman began to wear less restrictive clothing (shorter skirts and sleeveless tops).

They were also more active out-of-doors. Suntans were said to give ladies a glowing, healthier looking complexion.

This attitude persisted until the late 1990's when researchers found that 90% of skin cancer was caused by exposure to ultraviolet (UV) rays of the sun.

The most serious type of skin cancer, according to the Mayo Clinic, is melanoma. It develops in the cells (melanocytes) that produces melanin – the pigment that gives the skin its color. Melanoma can also form in your eyes and, rarely, in your internal organs, such as your intestines.

The exact cause of all melanomas isn't clear, but exposure to ultraviolet (UV) radiation from sunlight or tanning lamps and beds increases your risk of developing melanoma.

The risk of melanoma seems to be increasing in people under the age of 40, especially women. Knowing the warning signs of skin cancer can help ensure that cancerous changes are detected and treated before the cancer spreads. Melanoma can be treated successfully if it is detected early.

Factors that may increase your risk of melanoma include:

* Fair skin.
* A history of sunburns.
* Excessive ultraviolet (UV) light exposure – sun, tanning lights and beds.
* Living closer to the equator or at a higher elevation.
* Having over 50 moles or having unusual larger than normal moles or ones with irregular borders or a mixture of colors.
* A family history of melanoma.
* Weakened immune system. People who undergo organ transplants.

The American Cancer Society predicts 76,380 new cases of invasive melanoma will be diagnosed in the United States in 2016. Of those diagnosed, 10,130 will die, 6,750 men and 3,380 women.

Members of our family avoid the sun as much as possible, and visit a dermatologist every six months We try to follow as many of the Melanoma Guidelines listed on the next page, as we can. It sounds like a lot of work, but believe me, after losing Scott, the precautions are worth it.

Barbara Ann Carle

Melanoma Prevention Guidelines:

***Seek the shade**. Especially between 10 AM and 4 PM
***Do not burn**.
***Avoid tanning** and never use UV tanning beds.
***Cover up** with clothing, including a broad-brimmed hat and UV- blocking sunglasses.
***Use a broad spectrum (UVA/UVB) sunscreen** with a SPF of 15 or higher every day. For extended outdoor activity, use a water resistant, broad spectrum (UVA/UVB) sunscreen with an SPF of 30 or higher.
***Apply 1 ounce** (2 tablespoons) of sunscreen to your entire body 30 minutes before going outside. Reapply every two hours or immediately after swimming or excessive sweating.
***Keep newborns out of the sun**. Sunscreen should be used on babies over the age of six months.
***Examine your skin** head to toe every month.
***See your physician every year** for a professional skin exam.

Additional information about Melanoma is available from the American Cancer Society, M. D. Anderson Cancer Center and Mayo Clinic websites.

Acknowledgement

In one of the first creative writing classes I attended, the teacher said "Most people assume writing is a solitary endeavor. They imagine climbing the stairs to a dingy garret somewhere, preferably in Paris, living on bread and water, and after several years, emerging clutching the Great American novel. But the truth is writing is a team sport." We all laughed but, honestly, I didn't really understand what he meant.

That wonderful, wise teacher, Max Regan, introduced me to a community of amazing writers from whom I have learned so much. The members of the Spectrum Center Writer's Guild, Rosa Glenn Reilly, Melanie Miller, Ellen Seaton, Diana Galindo, Kirsten Cerre and Ron Bueker supported me with thoughtful suggestion and gentle critiques. And when the memories became too painful, they were quick with a large box of tissues and, much needed hugs.

I also want to send my appreciate to the many members of Max's ten-day Writing Projects Retreats in Boulder, Colorado. Whenever I attend, I return to Houston enriched by your talent.

Over the years, Max Regan became my Team Leader, mentor and my dear friend. He inspired, encouraged and showed me how this collection of poems could tell the story of my son Scott's brave battle with cancer.

Other teachers I would like to thank are Sarah Cortez, Dr. John Gorman of the Galveston Roundtable and Mary Margaret Carlisle of Gulf Coast Poets.

I am also grateful to my own personal team of wonderful fellow poets who helped me shape many of these poems, Rosa Glenn Reilly, Susan Gordon, Kay Cox, Germaine Welch, Loueva Smith, the late Robin McCorquodale, Stan Crawford, Matt Krohn, William Guest, Oscar Peña, Mary Ann Goodwin, Laura Peña, Sharon Goodwin, Diana Dettling Buckley, our beloved Billie McCauley, also my friends Roger Roffman, Mark Wood, Ruth Stevenson and Becky Newberry.

I would also like to send my sincere thanks to the doctors, nurses and staff of M. D. Anderson Cancer Center for the wonderful care, comfort and treatment they provided Scott during his illness. The assistance and support they offered our family, during this painful ordeal, will always be remembered and appreciated.

Of course, none of this would have been possible without the love and support of my husband Ed. He lived every moment of this book by my side. He held me up when I thought I couldn't take another step and has been my strength. Our three children Paula, Melissa and Glen traveled this journey along with us and they are always a source of love and inspiration.

I also want to recognize my daughter-in-law Carolyn Carle, who was widowed at such a young age. She went on to build a new life, as a single working mother, raising four young children. She has, amazingly, devoted her professional career to assisting families of terminally ill patients arrange for hospice care.

I have been blessed with the love of my six wonderful grandchildren, Joshua Haise, Emily Haise, Sarah Haise, Adam Van Dorn and my small but devoted fan club, Rose Carle and Scotty McDaniel.

Barbara Ann Carle is a poet, novelist and essay writer.

Her poems have appeared in various publications including the 2009 Poetry Society of Texas - Book of the Year, where her poem "The Battle" won the Ted O. Badger Award, the 2011, 2012 and 2013 Texas Poetry Calendars, the 2012 Summer Edition of Rattle Magazine and the 2016 Mutabilis Press anthology "Untameable City". Her first poetry book "New York Rhapsody", a collection of poems about growing up in New York City before and right after World War II, was published in 2009.

Barbara's essays have been published in numerous anthologies including "Thanksgiving to Christmas, a Patchwork of Stories", "That Thing We Do", "Fearless Nest" and five Chicken Soup books, "The Chocolate Lover's Soul', "Democrat's Soul", Republican's Soul", "Grieving and Recovery" and "It's Christmas". Her latest book "The Viking Ship", a collection of essays about her son Scott, will be available in the fall of 2017.

She is a member of the Spectrum Center's Writer's Guild, Gulf Coast Poets, The Poetry Society of Texas, The Divas of the Written Word and Women in the Visual and Literary Arts.

Barbara was born and raised in New York City but has been a Texas transplant since 1965. She is a retired police officer, the mother of four and the grandmother of six. Barbara lives in a high-rise in downtown Houston with her husband, Ed, where she is presently working on a new novel.

www.ingramcontent.com/pod-product-compliance
Lightning Source LLC
Chambersburg PA
CBHW060340050426
42449CB00011B/2800